Trucks

by Dee Ready

Content Consultant:
Suzanne Matthews
Chief of Staff
American Trucking Association

Bridgestone Books
an imprint of Capstone Press

Bridgestone Books are published by Capstone Press
818 North Willow Street, Mankato, Minnesota 56001
http://www.capstone-press.com

Library of Congress Cataloging-in-Publication Data
Ready, Dee.
    Trucks/by Dee Ready.
    p. cm.
    Includes bibliographical references and index.
    Summary: Describes various kinds of trucks, including garbage trucks, tow trucks,
and tankers.
    ISBN 1-56065-613-1
    1. Trucks--Juvenile literature. [1. Trucks.] I. Title.
TL230.15.R43   1998
629.224--dc21

                                                         97-12195
                                                            CIP
                                                             AC

Photo credits
Cheryl Blair, 18
Betty Crowell, 10
Dodge, 8
FPG/Laurance Aiuppy, 4; Ed Taylor, 6
International Stock/Elliott Varner Smith, 20
Lynn M. Stone, cover
Unicorn Stock/Jean Higgins, 12; Eric Berndt, 14; Shellie Nelson, 16

Table of Contents

Trucks

Trucks are used for many different jobs. They are made to carry things or pull things. Some people drive trucks for their jobs. Other people drive trucks for fun.

Jeeps

A jeep can drive where there are no roads. It has four-wheel drive. This means the front wheels pull the jeep. And the back wheels push the jeep. A jeep is strong enough to pull things, too.

Pickup Trucks

A pickup truck is a small truck. It has an open back called a bed. Many people drive pickups instead of cars. They use pickups to move or carry things.

Dump Trucks

A dump truck carries dirt and sand in its
bed. It moves the dirt to another place.
A machine lifts the front part of the bed.
The dirt slides out of the back of the truck.

Garbage Trucks

A garbage truck picks up garbage from bins and cans. Garbage is anything that is thrown away. The garbage goes into the back of the truck. A machine pushes the garbage deep inside the truck.

Cement Trucks

A cement truck has a round mixer. The mixer spins to mix cement. Cement is used to make roads and sidewalks. The cement comes out of a pipe. The pipe is in the back of the cement mixer.

Tow Trucks

A tow truck pulls cars that cannot be driven. It also pulls other trucks. A tow truck has a hook and a cable. The hook holds onto a car to pull it. The tow truck takes the car to be fixed.

Semi Trucks

A semi truck has a big trailer. The trailer is made to be pulled. It is used to carry things. Sometimes semis are called 18-wheelers. This is because many semis have 18 wheels.

Tanker Trucks

A tanker truck pulls a shiny, round tank. The tank looks like a large can on its side. It holds liquids like oil and gas. The liquid comes off the truck in a pipe.

Hands On: Big and Small Wheels

Trucks have big wheels. This makes them travel well over uneven ground. Small wheels drop into holes. This makes the ride bumpy. Big wheels ride over holes. This makes the ride more even.

What You Need:

An empty egg carton
A ping-pong ball
A baseball

What You Do:

1. Open the egg carton. Use the bottom part of the carton. This is the part where the eggs sit. It is your road.
2. Roll the ping-pong ball over the egg carton. See how it drops into the holes. The ping-pong ball is like a small wheel. The ride is bumpy.
3. Now roll the baseball over the egg carton. It rolls over the holes. The baseball is like a big wheel. The ride is even.

Words to Know

cement (suh-MENT)—a gray paste used to make sidewalks and roads

four-wheel drive (FOR-WEEL DRIVE)— all four wheels move the truck. The front wheels pull the truck. The back wheels push the truck.

garbage (GAR-bij)—anything that is thrown away

liquid (LIK-wid)—something wet that you can pour like oil or gas

Read More

Crews, Donald. *Truck*. New York: Greenwillow Books, 1980.

Oliver, Stephen. *Trucks*. Eye Openers. New York: Little Simon, 1991.

Strickland, Paul. *All About Trucks*. Milwaukee: Gareth Stevens, 1990.

Wolfe, Robert L. *The Truck Book*. Minneapolis: Carolrhoda Books, 1981.

Internet Sites

The Pickup Truck Homepage
http://www.rtd.com/~mlevine/pickup.html
Truckers.com
http://www.truckers.com

Index